The Boomslang Snake

Alicia Z. Klepeis

New York

Published in 2018 by Cavendish Square Publishing, LLC
243 5th Avenue, Suite 136, New York, NY 10016

Copyright © 2018 by Cavendish Square Publishing, LLC

First Edition

No part of this publication may be reproduced, stored in a retrieval system, or transmitted in any form or by any means—electronic, mechanical, photocopying, recording, or otherwise—without the prior permission of the copyright owner. Request for permission should be addressed to Permissions, Cavendish Square Publishing, 243 5th Avenue, Suite 136, New York, NY 10016. Tel (877) 980-4450; fax (877) 980-4454.

Website: cavendishsq.com

This publication represents the opinions and views of the author based on his or her personal experience, knowledge, and research. The information in this book serves as a general guide only. The author and publisher have used their best efforts in preparing this book and disclaim liability rising directly or indirectly from the use and application of this book.

CPSIA Compliance Information: Batch #CS17CSQ

All websites were available and accurate when this book was sent to press.

Library of Congress Cataloging-in-Publication Data

Names: Klepeis, Alicia Z.
Title: The boomslang snake / Alicia Z. Klepeis.
Description: New York : Cavendish Square Publishing, 2018. | Series: Toxic creatures | Includes index.
Identifiers: ISBN 9781502625977 (pbk.) | ISBN 9781502625892 (library bound) | ISBN 9781502625816 (6 pack) | ISBN 9781502625847 (ebook)
Subjects: LCSH: Poisonous snakes--Juvenile literature.
Classification: LCC QL666.O6 K55 2018 | DDC 597.96--dc23

Editorial Director: David McNamara
Editor: Fletcher Doyle
Copy Editor: Nathan Heidelberger
Associate Art Director: Amy Greenan
Designer: Alan Sliwinski
Production Coordinator: Karol Szymczuk
Photo Research: J8 Media

The photographs in this book are used by permission and through the courtesy of: Cover Mattias Klum/National Geographic Magazines/Getty Images; Throughout book, Deliverance/Shutterstock.com; p. 4 Petra Christen/Shutterstock.com; p. 6 Jurie Maree/iStock; p. 7 Mark Boulton/Alamy Stock Photo; p. 8 Hoberman Collection/Universal Images Group/Getty Images; p. 9 Stuart G Porter/Shutterstock.com; p. 10 Austin J. Stevens/Animals Animals; p. 13 Opka/Shutterstock.com; p. 14 Chris Harvey/ardea.com/Pantheon/Superstock; p. 16 Duncan Noakes/YAY Micro/age footstock; p. 17 NoPainNoGain/Shutterstock.com; p. 18 Jegelewicz/Wikimedia Commons/File:Karl Patterson Schmidt.jpg/CC BY-SA 3.0; p. 22 Humpata/iStock/Thinkstock; p. 24 Gerard Lacz/Animals Animals; p. 26 Deshakalyan Chowdhury/AFP/Getty Images; p. 27 Joyce Marshall/The Fort Worth Star-Telegram/AP Photo.

Printed in the United States of America

CONTENTS

1 Basics of Boomslangs 5

　Boomslang Snake Quick Facts 12

2 Boomslangs and Their Venom 15

3 Balance of Nature 23

　Toxic Creatures Quiz 28

　Glossary 29

　Find Out More 30

　Index 31

　About the Author 32

A boomslang snake looks out from its perch in a tree in Botswana.

Basics of Boomslangs

From its appearance to its venom, the boomslang snake is one amazing animal. These snakes are **arboreal.** They make their homes in trees and shrubs. They live in Africa, south of the Sahara desert.

Boomslangs can thrive in different habitats. They live in savannas and lowland forests. They also live in grasslands and semidesert areas known as karoos.

Hard to See

Boomslang snakes are **diurnal**. They are active during the day. They spend most of their time in the trees. Boomslangs are excellent at hiding. They slither along branches until they find a good hiding place. They will travel to the ground for food or to **bask** in the sun. A boomslang may head to ground level in search of **prey**. However, it will climb back up a tree to eat its food.

This boomslang snake, with its blueish-green color, blends in among the leaves in its environment.

A boomslang snake opens its mouth wide to eat a chameleon in Zambia.

Boomslangs are carnivores (meat eaters). Their diet is made up mainly of small tree-dwelling lizards and frogs. They often eat chameleons. Sometimes they eat small mammals, birds, and the eggs of birds and reptiles. Boomslangs have been known to eat other boomslangs.

Boomslangs prey on many animals, and they have many **predators**. Besides other boomslangs, these snakes are also eaten by large meat-eating birds.

Boomslang snakes are not large. Adults are usually between 3 and 5 feet (0.9 to 1.5 meters) long. In some parts of their range, they can be more than 6 feet (1.8 m) long. These snakes have

A brown snake eagle is one type of bird that preys on boomslang snakes.

The eyes of this juvenile boomslang snake seem quite large compared to its head.

slender bodies. At birth, boomslangs are about 1 foot (30 centimeters) long. These **hatchlings** look somewhat cartoonlike. Why? They are skinny with bright green eyes that take up much of their heads.

Not all boomslangs are the same color. Males tend to be bright green. Females are more of a dull olive brown. Young boomslangs are more colorful than adults. They often have a stripe down their back. This stripe usually fades as they become adults.

Females Lay Eggs

In their native lands, breeding season is from July to early October. During this time, male boomslangs may fight each other. They are trying to gain the

A young boomslang lies among a clutch of eggs about to hatch.

right to mate with a female. After mating, there is a **gestation** period of about sixty days. Boomslang snakes are **oviparous**. That means they lay eggs. A female will usually lay between eight and twenty-seven eggs. The eggs have soft shells. They are about the size of ping-pong balls.

Boomslangs lay their eggs in damp places, like a tree hollow, so they don't dry out. In about sixty-five to one hundred days, the eggs will hatch.

Boomslang snakes are deadly from the time they are born. Even hatchlings can deliver lethal doses of venom. So unless another boomslang or a big meat-eating bird attacks, these snakes are not very vulnerable. Boomslangs are shy. They prefer to avoid conflict. On average, boomslangs live about eight years in the wild.

Boomslangs are the only **species** in their genus, *Dispholidus*. So they are truly one of a kind!

Boomslang Snake Quick Facts

Scientific name: *Dispholidus typus*

Common name: Boomslang; *Boomslang* in the Afrikaans language of southern Africa means "tree snake."

Size: Usually 3–5 feet (0.9–1.5 m) as adults, but can be more than 6 feet (1.8 m) long.

Coloration: The boomslang is one of the few snakes in which color is different between males and females (sexual dichromatism). Birds such as cardinals share this trait. Females are usually brown, and males have brighter colors.

Deadly Venom: The boomslang carries only 4 to 8 milligrams (0.0008 to 0.0016 teaspoons) of venom, but as little as 5 milligrams (0.001 tsp) can kill a human.

Fun Fact: Boomslang snakes have excellent sight but are color-blind.

Big bite: The boomslang delivers venom with fangs (3 to 5 millimeters, or less than 0.2 inches, long) located in the back of its mouth. It can open its mouth 170 degrees so it can bite arms and legs.

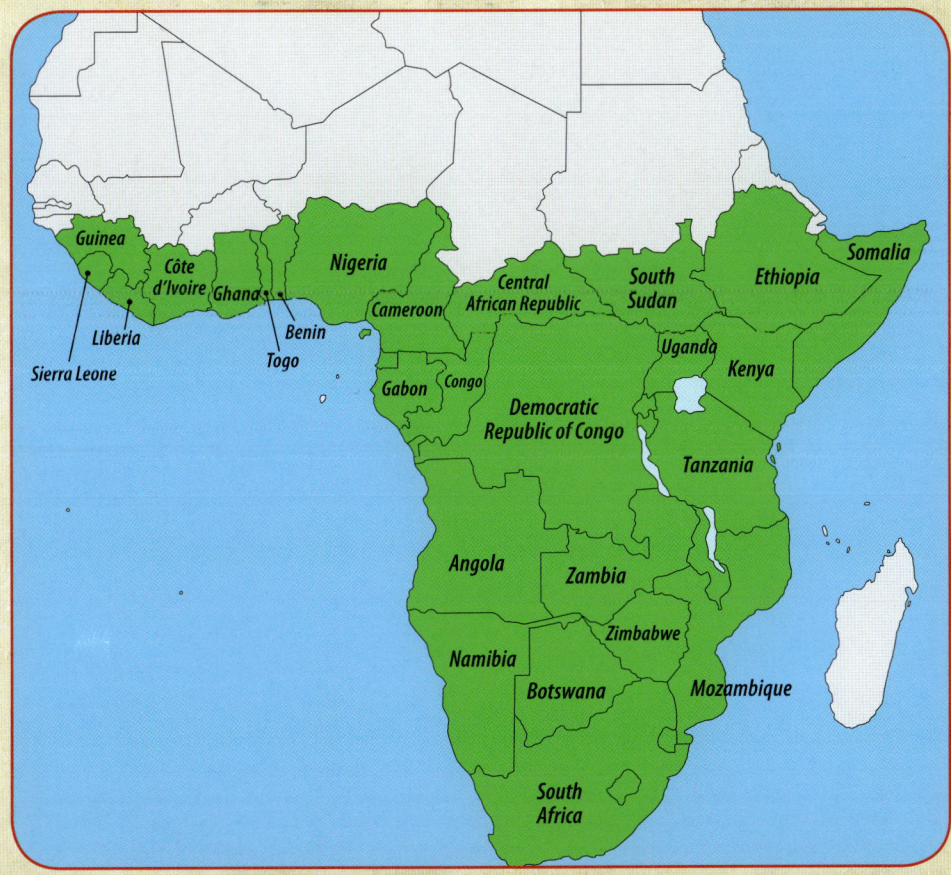

This map of Africa marks the countries where boomslang snakes are found in green.

This boomslang snake is in a threatening pose.

Boomslangs and Their Venom

Many people think boomslang snakes are scary. After all, they are venomous. Venomous animals can inject venom into their prey. How? Some use fangs. Others use stingers or spines. This is different from being poisonous. Poisonous animals make toxins that are harmful when eaten or touched.

Boomslangs make their own venom. They do this with glands that evolved from salivary glands. (These are the ones humans use to make spit.) The venom is stored in a sac inside the snake's head. It stays there until the snake bites its prey.

Fangs in Back

Boomslangs are rear-fanged snakes. At the rear of their jaws, they have enlarged teeth (fangs). Most rear-fanged snakes have short fangs. The boomslangs' fangs are longer than most rear-fanged

This boomslang is flashing it fangs. From this position, the snake could easily get hold of its prey.

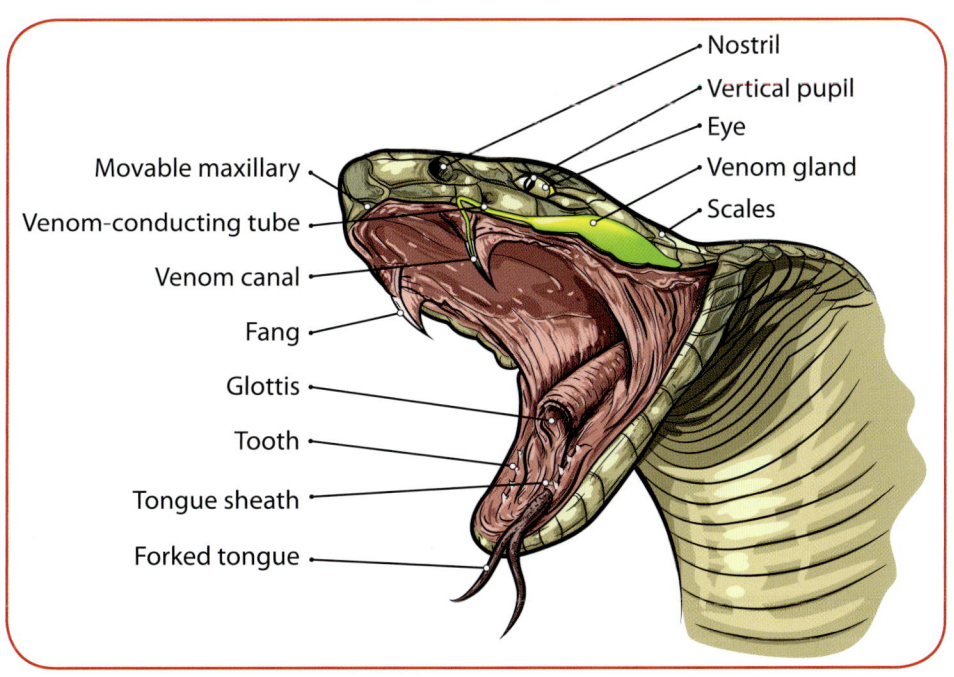

This diagram shows the parts of a snake's head, from its forked tongue to its venom glands.

snakes. The fangs have grooves; the venom runs down these grooves. These snakes can open their mouths really wide—to about 170 degrees! This allows the boomslang to chomp down on a victim's leg, arm, or shoulder. A boomslang may strike a few times. Why? To be sure enough venom has gotten into its prey.

Karl P. Schmidt's Terrifying Discovery

In 1957, snake expert Karl Schmidt was working at the Field Museum in Chicago. While examining a young boomslang snake, he was bitten on his thumb. At the time, rear-fanged snakes were not considered dangerous. Schmidt didn't seek treatment, but he wrote down his symptoms. The next day, he died from the snake's venom.

This drawing of Karl Schmidt is based on a photograph.

Then the venom does its work. Nasty work. Boomslang venom does not act fast. What happens if a person is bitten by a boomslang? It can take several hours—even up to a day—for the effects of the venom to show up.

Scientists use the LD50 test to compare boomslang venom with other snakes' venom. Animals, usually mice, are injected with venom. The amount of venom that kills half of 1 kilogram (2.2 pounds) of the animals gives the LD50 figure. (LD stands for "lethal dose.") Venom has been tested from many kinds of snakes. Boomslang venom usually ranks in the top ten.

A boomslang injects between 1.6 and 8.0 milligrams of venom per bite. Fifty mice weigh a total of 1 kilogram. A dose of 0.07 mg of its venom kills half of the fifty mice. This means the boomslang has enough venom to kill half of a group of 6,667 mice!

How much boomslang venom is needed to kill a person? Five milligrams of venom could kill a human. That's one one-thousandth of a teaspoon!

Venom Changes Blood

Not all snake venom is the same. Different types lead to different health problems. A neurotoxin from a cobra or a mamba will disrupt nerve signals. This causes muscles and organs such as the lungs to stop working. A cytotoxin from a rattlesnake or a viper will destroy cells in your body. Organs such as the heart can be severely damaged. Boomslang venom is **hemotoxic**. This venom affects the blood of prey (human or animal). It causes red blood cells to rupture. This leads to lots of internal bleeding. Hemotoxins can also disrupt the ability for blood to **clot.** When blood clots, it gets thick and bleeding stops. Hemotoxins also can cause damage to prey's tissues and organs.

Boomslang venom acts slowly, so victims sometimes do not realize they need to rush for medical help. Victims may have headaches and nausea. They may feel sleepy. But the venom basically causes the victim to bleed to death. Even a small scratch will bleed heavily. People who were bitten can bleed from their nostrils and gums. They will bleed in their urine and feces. Some victims' bodies take on a bluish tinge because of all the internal bleeding. Many also say they see with a yellow tinge. This could be due to bleeding inside their eyes. It's a horrible way to die.

Boomslang venom is super toxic, so it's a good thing that these snakes are shy. Fewer than ten reported deaths from their bites have been recorded worldwide. There is boomslang antivenom available. If given on time, it can counteract the effects of the venom.

A boomslang preys on a young bird in southern Africa. It eats the head first.

Balance of Nature

Boomslangs are toxic creatures. They frighten people all over Africa. Do they have any benefits for us or the world at large? Most scientists would say they do. All animals are important to the ecosystems where they live. This is even true for venomous ones.

Boomslangs are part of the food web. They eat lizards, birds, and other small animals. Some of the rodents they eat can destroy crops. These rodents also carry disease, so reducing their numbers is good for farmers and others who live near boomslangs.

Larger carnivorous birds eat boomslangs. Ospreys and secretary birds prey on them. So do falcons, kestrels, and other diurnal raptors. Boomslangs eat one another. It seems they can be hurt by their own type of venom.

A common kestrel, which is known to eat boomslangs, perches with its meal in Kenya's Masai Mara Park.

Snakes Fear Humans

Boomslangs also fear humans and keep away from them. They can sense a human long before a human can see them. When you approach a boomslang, it will get away before you even know it's there. Most attacks by boomslangs only happen when people try to capture or kill them.

Boomslang venom can be useful to researchers. But boomslang venom is hard to get. Specially trained snake handlers have to first catch these shy snakes. Then they have to "milk" the snakes. Handlers do this by using their forefingers and thumbs to carefully grab the back of the snake's head. While in this position, they can press on the snake's venom glands. A handler must keep the snake from turning its head and biting. The venom gets squeezed into a container. It takes the venom of many snakes to have enough to work with.

A trained snake handler collects venom from a Russell's viper. This venom will be used to make antivenom.

The collected venom is used to make an antivenom that saves lives every year. This antivenom is the only known way to cure a bite victim. Giving the patient fresh blood and **plasma** is also helpful to recovery.

South African researchers have been important in the study of boomslangs and their venom. Future research may make it cheaper to produce boomslang antivenom. This could help make it more available to Africans who live in rural areas where the snakes live.

Boomslang snakes are not endangered. Their populations seem to be healthy throughout their range. Hopefully snake experts will continue to learn more about these toxic creatures.

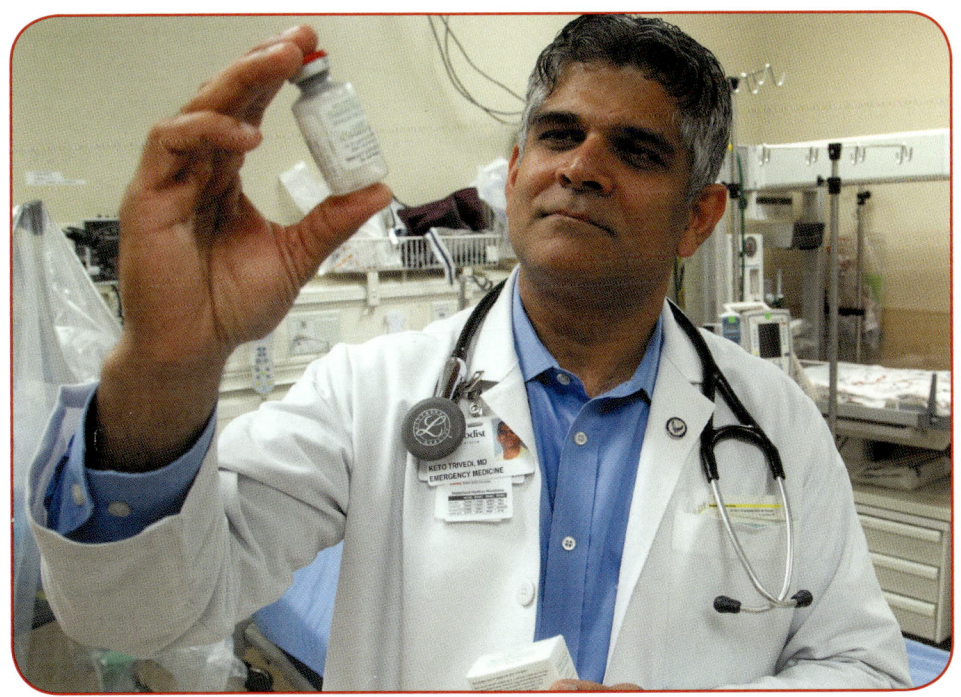

Dr. Keto Trivedi holds a bottle of antivenom available for snakebite victims at a Texas hospital.

Toxic Creatures Quiz

1. What do boomslangs eat?

2. What kind of fangs do boomslangs have?

3. What does boomslang venom do to victims?

4. What benefits do boomslangs have for the world?

Answer Key

1. Boomslangs are meat eaters. They often eat frogs, lizards, chameleons, and even small mammals. They sometimes eat birds and the eggs of birds and lizards.

2. Boomslangs are rear-fanged. Boomslang fangs are solid. They have a groove for the venom to run down into prey.

3. Boomslang venom affects blood. This venom causes red blood cells to rupture and prevents clotting. It also damages the prey's tissues and organs. Victims typically bleed to death.

4. They are an important part of the food web where they live, and they can control the population of animals that are a nuisance, like rodents. Scientists can make antivenom from them to help bite victims.

arboreal Living or usually found in trees.

bask To lie exposed to light and warmth, usually from the sun.

clot When blood gets thick and partly solid so bleeding stops.

diurnal Active mainly in the daytime.

gestation The period of carrying young before birth or before eggs are laid.

hatchling A recently hatched animal, such as a snake.

hemotoxic Capable of causing damage to red blood cells.

oviparous Producing young by means of laying eggs.

plasma The colorless fluid in blood that carries blood cells.

predator An animal that lives by killing and eating other animals.

prey An animal hunted or killed by another animal for food.

species Living organisms made up of similar individuals capable of producing fertile offspring.

Books

Harris, Terrell. *Venomous Snakes*. New York: Gareth Stevens Publishing, 2010.

Morgan, Michaela. *The Deadly Boomslang*. New York: Oxford University Press, 2014.

Websites

National Geographic—Boomslang vs. Chameleon

http://video.nationalgeographic.com/video/boomslang_stalkschameleon

This website features a video showing the boomslang in its natural habitat and also catching a chameleon.

Reptiles Magazine—The Boomslang Snake Of Africa

http://www.reptilesmagazine.com/Venomous-Snakes/Boomslang-Snake-Of-Africa

This website tells the story of how it was discovered that boomslangs were toxic, their hunting methods, and how they deliver their venom.

Page numbers in **boldface** are illustrations. Entries in **boldface** are glossary terms.

antivenom, 21, 26–27, **27**
arboreal, 5
bask, 6
birds, 7–8, **8**, 11–12, **22**, 23–24, **24**
chameleons, 7, **7**
clot, 20
color, 10, 12
diurnal, 6, 24
fangs, 13, 15–18, **16**, **17**
food web, 23–24

gestation, 11
glands, 15–16, **17**, 25
habitat, 5, **13**
hatchling, 9, **9**, **10**, 11
hemotoxic, 20
LD50 test, 19
oviparous, 11
plasma, 26
predator, 8
prey, 6, 8, 15–17, 20, 24
reproduction, 10–11
Schmidt, Karl, 18, **18**
species, 11
symptoms, 18, 20–21
venom, 5, 11–13, 15–21, 24–26, **26**

ABOUT THE AUTHOR

From amazing animals to jellybeans, **Alicia Z. Klepeis** loves to research fun and out-of-the-ordinary topics that make nonfiction exciting for readers. Alicia began her career at the National Geographic Society. She is the author of numerous children's books, including *Bizarre Things We've Called Medicine*, *Brain Eaters: Creatures with Zombielike Diets*, and *The World's Strangest Foods*. She once saw a taipan snake at Sydney's Toronga Zoo. Alicia lives with her family in upstate New York.